ILLUSTRATED TALES OF
WILTSHIRE

EDDY GREENFIELD

AMBERLEY

Acknowledgements

As I write this book Covid-19 is still very much with us, and there is discussion about the so-called Indian (or Delta) variant starting to gain a foothold in parts of the UK, so being able to travel around freely to gain the illustrations for this book in person has simply not been possible. It has also meant that images that I initially desired to use were not always forthcoming. I therefore wish to give my most grateful thanks and gratitude to all those who have made available the public domain and Creative Commons images that have been used in this book. Without them, *Illustrated Tales of Wiltshire* would simply not have been possible.

First published 2023

Amberley Publishing
The Hill, Stroud
Gloucestershire, GL5 4EP

www.amberley-books.com

British Library Cataloguing in Publication Data.
A catalogue record for this book is available from the British Library.

ISBN 978 1 3981 1126 4 (paperback)
ISBN 978 1 3981 1127 1 (ebook)

Typesetting by SJmagic DESIGN SERVICES, India.
Printed in Great Britain.

Contents

Introduction

It is impossible to travel anywhere in Wiltshire without being awed by the standing stones, barrows and hillforts that litter this county; it seems that almost every stone, lump, bump, and high ground is imbued with its own folklore and legends. Yet, the county is also just as famous for its modern links to the armed forces, whether that is the expanse of Salisbury Plain or the MoD bases at

Map of Wiltshire. (OpenStreetMap)

Boscombe Down or Porton Down. These, in turn, have spawned many modern urban legends and rumours of secret experiments. It is no wonder that with such a wealth of ancient wonders juxtaposed with more recent history that Wiltshire is home to so many myths, legends and stories.

New and old will be explored in this book, from origin stories of some of the many landscape features and stone circles, to famous (and infamous) personalities, peculiar artefacts and strange stories. From local customs and superstitions to mysterious landmarks and memorials, we are about to take a journey into the unknown.

Our whistle-stop tour is going to be a bumpy one; we are going to climb hills and dive down valleys, sweep across plains and dig deep into the shadows. So, be sure to hold on tight as we delve into the strange and unusual worlds where the realms of fact and fiction merge in the mists that swirl in that mystical twilight zone and nothing is quite as it appears. Are you ready? Here we go!

Magic Water

Wiltshire is no stranger to sacred springs and holy wells, but the one at Purton Stoke – known as Salt Hole – has perhaps the most fascinating history. The spring water that bubbled up through the ground here has been a source of water – particularly by the labourers – since the Middle Ages, if not before. The history of the water's supposed medicinal properties is similarly ancient.

The spring first came to wider prominence in the nineteenth century when the then owner, Dr Samuel Sadler, had the spring blocked off, and even attempted to bury it, to prevent people from trespassing across his land. The story goes that Dr Sadler, like most other doctors, was sceptical of any healing powers of the water, but in around 1860 he fell ill and finally partook of the spring. A miraculous cure soon followed and he had a pump house built at Salt Hole in order to draw the water, bottle it and sell it commercially as a cure-all, particularly in relation to digestive complaints, liver and kidney ailments, joint and muscle problems, bronchial illnesses, nervous conditions and as a pick-me-up for those with general malaise.

Later owners of the land continued to sell the water well into the 1920s, and many attempted to develop 'Purton Spa' into a health resort but to no avail. Nonetheless, until healthcare became available to all in 1948, vendors would bottle Purton's healing water and travel across large parts of north Wiltshire peddling the miracle cure in the streets.

River Key, close to Salt Hole Spa. (Wayland Smith)

2

The Flying Monk

The Wright brothers famously made the world's first powered flight in 1903 after having spent several years experimenting with gliders. Then, on 27 June 1909 the world's first soaring flight in a glider was made at Amberley in West Sussex, when seventeen-year-old Eric Gordon-England flew for almost a minute and gained a height of 50 feet in a specially built glider designed by the French artist Jose Weiss. However, it was a Wiltshire holy man that perhaps made the first flight in Britain – according to a twelfth-century tale.

According to William of Malmesbury (the resident historian and librarian of Malmesbury Abbey), Eilmer – a monk at Malmesbury – believed that human flight was possible and in the first decade of the eleventh century built a primitive

Malmesbury Abbey's west tower. (Ethan Doyle White)

'glider' after observing how birds could maintain flight by making use of the air currents. Once completed, he took the machine to the top of the west tower. This glider would appear to simply have been a pair of artificial wings or kite-like device strapped to the arms and legs, but, sure as to its effectiveness, Eilmer leaped off the tower and caught the wind under his contraption. William says that the monk flew around 200 metres until the turbulence became too great and Eilmer became suddenly aware of his predicament and plummeted like a stone, breaking both his legs in the untimely landing. The monk, it is claimed, put the failure of his aircraft down to not having added a tail to stabilise it in flight, and spent the rest of his life crippled by his injuries.

Despite this, William related how Eilmer was not put off the dream of flight, and petitioned the abbot to try again, but was refused permission.

Much of the abbey was destroyed in 1500 when the spire collapsed, but part of the building was later restored and turned into a church. A modern stained-glass window commemorating Eilmer and his flying machine has been installed in one of the chapels.

Eilmer's window. (Arpingstone)

3
Killed by a Tyger

Malmesbury Abbey also has another interesting memorial. In the corner of the churchyard is a headstone erected in memory of Hannah Twynnoy, who died on 23 October 1703 at the age of thirty-three. The inscription records the unusual fate that led to Hannah's demise:

> In bloom of life
> She's snatched from hence,
> She had not room
> To make defence;
> For Tyger fierce
> Took Life away
> And here she lies
> In a bed of Clay,
> Until the Resurrection Day.

The question is what was a tiger doing in a small Wiltshire town? In 1703, Hannah was working as a maid at the White Lion Inn in Gloucester Street. In the rear yard was an early travelling menagerie – an old attraction that has thankfully

Hannah Twynnoy's grave. (Rob Farrow)

long since been confined to history – exhibiting several exotic animals for patrons of the pub to pay to see. Hannah appears to have had a particular attraction to the tiger, which had been tethered to the ground, and she is said to have teased the poor animal in spite of repeated warnings from the handlers.

Sadly for Hannah, the tether was not particularly strong and, ignoring the warnings, continued to harass the tiger. As any creature would when subjected to such behaviour, the tiger reached his limit and lunged at her, pulling his restraints out of the ground and mauled the girl with his enormous paws.

Former White Lion Inn. (Jaggery)

4

The Malmesbury Witches

In the 1670s, Malmesbury was supposedly in the grips of an entire coven of witches, numbering fourteen people in total, who were said to terrorise the town's inhabitants with their evil deeds.

The history of alleged witchcraft in the town dated back to the 1630s, when 'John Barlowe's wife' was convicted and executed in around 1636. Later, during the English Civil War, the local area was under the control of the Parliamentarian army in 1643, and the soldiers stationed at Westport so ill-treated Alice Elgar that she poisoned herself; her body was buried at a local crossroads. Elgar was alleged to have some involvement in witchcraft, as was a long-standing friend of hers – a widow named Orchard. The latter's story occurred around twenty years later when she visited the house of Hugh Bartholomew in Malmesbury to ask for some yeast. His wife, Mary, believed that if the old woman was helped, then the family would be bewitched; Mary refused any help. Orchard left, but was heard to mutter to herself as she did. Soon afterwards, a large wooden money chest upstairs was heard to crash to the floor. Hugh believed that Orchard had sent spirits into the house to steal his money and gave chase. Arriving at Orchard's cottage, she informed him that no such thing had happened; the nails had simply fallen out of the chest and not a single coin was missing. Hugh returned home and found that, indeed, the nails were missing, but all the coins were present, having been spilled across the floor.

Orchard left town and was not heard of until four months later, when she was in Salisbury Gaol for bewitching a young maid at Burbage, near Marlborough. In this case, she is said to have arrived at the maid's house and asked for some food. The maid had spent a busy day working in the garden and said that she would provide a meal, but first she would wash and fix a meal for herself. The maid's father took pity on the old woman and desired that she be given some bread and cheese and be sent on her way; the maid stood firm and refused.

Orchard then trotted around the garden and then went into the middle of the circle she had just paced out, squatted, and muttered some words that the others present could not understand. She repeated this three times before departing. Meanwhile, the maid had fetched a bowl of water to wash her hands in, and in so doing her fingers suddenly burst into pain. Orchard was blamed and several labourers nearby gave chase. The woman was finally found three days later around 20 miles away and was taken to Eddington Manor; the lord of the manor listened to the complaint and ordered that she be sent to Salisbury. However, the head labourer desired that she first be taken back to Burbage. When they arrived, the maid was suffering terribly and was in a fit of fever. Orchard was brought in and

Site of Fisherton Gaol,
Salisbury. (Jim Osley)

was accused of witchcraft, for which she would hang. Orchard was unshaken and
replied that the maid's condition exists only because she had washed her hands
in 'unwholesome water'. If she washed again in 'wholesome water' she would be
cured. A fresh bowl of water was brought in, and Orchard made three circles in it
with her finger, declared it wholesome, and the maid dipped her hands in and was
instantly cured. Orchard was then taken to Salisbury, convicted, and hanged.

By the mid-1670s, Hugh Bartholomew had died, and Mary remarried Robert
Webb, an alderman of Malmesbury. A woman named Ann Tilling came to Mary
and confessed that she, Judith Witchell and Elizabeth Peacock were all witches
and had bewitched Mary's son, Thomas Webb. Thomas suddenly became plagued
by violent fits, up to three or four a day, between which he would suffer from
bursts of swearing and profanities against God. He could also speak with the
three women even though they were not present. Ann had been a good friend of
Mary and felt so wracked with guilt that she begged forgiveness, stating that she
had been forced into it by Witchell and Peacock.

Ann was taken before the magistrates and repeated her confession. She further
confessed that there were eleven other witches in the Malmesbury coven, and
that they all met regularly to feast, drink and plot against people in the town.

Upon these confessions, the alleged witches (two men and twelve women) were all arrested and tried before the town's justices. Just as preparations were being made to send them all to Salisbury Gaol for execution, another Justice of the Peace suddenly arrived, much to the chagrin of the other magistrates; however, they allowed him to sit on the case and urged him to read Ann's confession and hear twelve-year-old Thomas Webb's testimony. The new justice did so, but had serious concerns about the proceedings of the trial. He requested that he be allowed to make a statement before the accused were sent away.

The room was cleared of all but the justices and the 'gentlemen of quality'. The new justice (who left an anonymous letter about the events) announced that he believed that the fourteen were about to be committed for a serious crime upon little or no evidence; for all but Tilling, Witchell and Peacock, the charge was merely one of general suspicion of witchcraft, besides which a first conviction for such a crime should bear a sentence of standing in the pillory in four Wiltshire towns, and not an immediate capital conviction.

However, he also said that he saw no evidence whatsoever against Peacock – the alleged coven leader – and also urged that the boy's testimony be dismissed as either false or a result of madness brought on by the fits. Turning next to Ann's confession, he said that it was merely a conspiracy concocted by Ann, in confederacy with the boy's parents, to drag the other women into the matter. Both Witchell and Peacock were women of ill repute locally, and the latter had also only just recently been acquitted of witchcraft at another trial at Salisbury. He argued that eleven of the accused be discharged and released immediately, and Ann, Witchell and Peacock be held at Salisbury, but not to be subjected to torture. Meanwhile, the boy should be watched to see if his malady improves, and two ministers should regularly meet with Ann to see if her confession changed over time. The other justices gave their assent to these proposals.

Eventually, Peacock was acquitted again, but Judith Witchell and Ann Tilling were both hanged for witchcraft.

Former Malmesbury courthouse, closed *c.* 1616. (Steve Roberts)

5
The Mystery Mud Springs

From a field south of Royal Wootton Bassett cold, grey mud slowly oozes up out of three great 'blisters' measuring 10 metres long by 5 meters high, encased in a thin skin of marshland plants and vegetation in an otherwise flat landscape.

The phenomenon was first 'discovered' in 1974 when River Authority workmen were clearing a nearby stream and accidentally broke into the protective skin of one of these blisters, causing the liquid mud to pour out – since then mud has continued to seep out from fissures.

An attempt was made to fill in one of the blisters in 1990, but despite around 100 tonnes of material being poured into the blister, it didn't stop the liquid mud from oozing out. The springs then underwent scientific investigation in 1996, although much about them still remains a mystery.

The area around the springs is fenced off and signs warn against trespassing owing to risk of entrapment in the mud. The springs are said to be so deep that it has been claimed that cattle have disappeared after entering the area.

Canal near the mud springs. (Brian Robert Marshall)

6

Battle of Badon

Liddington Castle – an early Iron Age hillfort commanding the plains to the south-east of modern Swindon – is but one of several locations cited as being the site of Mount Badon, where a fierce battle was said to have been fought between the Britons and invading Anglo-Saxons at the very end of the Roman era. It is generally accepted by many to have been a real event, albeit greatly mythologised over the centuries and has been drawn into Arthurian legend.

The first recorded mention of the Battle of Badon was an early sixth-century text written by St Gildas concerning the history of Britain as the Roman era was coming to an end, and therefore written at least 100 years after the supposed battle was fought. Nonetheless, St Gildas describes how the Saxons swept across southern England before the leader of the British forces, Ambrosius Aurelianus, was able to regroup his shattered forces and mount an effective resistance.

Local tradition holds that the battle was fought at Liddington Castle, although other suggestions include Badbury Rings in Dorset, Bath, Little Solsbury Hill in Somerset, and even Bowden Hill in Scotland. A recent book by Andrew Breeze

Liddington Castle. (Mik Peach)

Ringsbury Camp. (Vieve Forward)

(*British Battles 493-937*) has also put forward Ringsbury Camp – around 11 miles north-east of Liddington Castle – as a suggestion.

Wherever it was fought, the battle was said to have been a major victory for the native Britons, and brought peace and prosperity to the entire kingdom for years to come. All mention of the battle goes quiet until the Venerable Bede briefly mentions it in passing around 200 years after St Gildas' work was written.

Until now, there had been no mention of King Arthur in the stories, but this changed in AD 828, when another purported history of the pre-Saxon Britons named him as the leader of the British forces at the battle – the twelfth great battle fought against the Saxons following their invasion. In this history, the Saxons are said to have lost 960 men in the battle, all of whom were struck down by King Arthur alone. From this point onwards, subsequent writers linked the Battle of Badon with the legend of King Arthur, and the stories become ever increasingly fictitious and mythologised.

Whether the Battle of Badon was real, and whether or not it was fought at Liddington Castle is up for debate, but Liddington did play an important role in a more recent war, however. The old hilltop was used as a night-time decoy during the Second World War, where a series of incendiary devices (controlled from a bunker atop the hill) were ignited to give the impression of a city on fire in order to draw German bombers away from their actual targets.

The Legend of the White Hand

The village of Draycot Cerne once had an ancient manor known as Draycot House, although a more recent manor house has been built on the site of the original. During the reign of King Henry VII, the house came into the possession of Sir Thomas Long on account of his mother being the sole heiress of the previous owner, the Wayte family. Sir Thomas married Margery Darrell, daughter of Sir George Darrell of Littlecote, and had three sons. It was through his eldest son, Henry, that Sir Thomas had a grandson named Walter Long, and it is Walter to whom the story concerns.

Walter had two wives during his lifetime, the second of whom was Catherine Thynne, daughter of Sir John Thynne of Longleat. The newlywed couple spent six weeks on honeymoon before returning back to Draycot House, where they were met by great merriment and revelry by the locals – all, that is, except one. The unhappy partygoer was John Long, Walter's son from his previous marriage and heir to his father's great estates at Draycot and Wraxhall.

John was said to be a kind and considerate gentleman, generous to his heart and never suspicious as to the motives of others; his new step-mother, however, was already scheming (if we are to believe the story). Lady Catherine and her brother, Sir Egremont, knew that John was the rightful heir to the wealth and fortune that they had just married into, and that any children that Catherine might have with Walter would not be entitled to any inheritance on account of being younger than John. Lady Catherine saw John as nothing more than an obstruction to the rights of her own future heirs and plotted John's downfall – at any cost, John must be ruined or so disgraced as to be disinherited.

Walter Long, like his son, was a highly generous and thoughtful man, and often bestowed large sums of money upon John, and it was this that Catherine and Sir Egremont recognised as their means to bring ruin upon the young heir. They both supplied John with even more money and gold and told him to enjoy life.

No matter how well-behaved a young man might be, when supplied with an endless stream of money there will come times when he will indulge himself to excess, and John was not immune to this side of human nature. Naturally, such tales would feed back to Lady Catherine, who would simply smile and excuse them. However, inside she kept a mental note of John's indulgences and exaggerated them into terrible crimes when she later related them to Walter. Sir Egremont would also pick Walter's brains about John's alleged behaviour in drinking and gambling, and upon his wife's advice agreed to rewrite his will to disinherit his son and making Lady Catherine and Sir Egremont the sole heirs to his estates.

Sir Walter had by now fallen gravely ill and it was Sir Egremont who drew up a new draft will, presented it to Walter for approval, and then had it copied and submitted to a clerk to have it officially written up legally.

It is now that the story takes a supernatural turn. While the clerk was writing up the new will on parchment – an act that required a good eye and bright light – he saw a ghostly white hand of a lady appear between the parchment and the light, but then it disappeared almost as soon as he noticed it. The clerk paused momentarily before continuing about his work, convinced it was just his imagination.

The hand appeared before his eyes once more as he reached the important clause – the one that disinherited John in a litany of slanderous accusations. The clerk let out a shriek of terror and rushed into Sir Egrmont's chambers to awaken him and tell him of what had just happened. He claimed that the ghostly hand was that of the late Lady Long – John's mother – who had returned from the dead to stop her son being wrongly treated.

Sir Egremont dismissed the clerk and appointed another to complete the work. The will was signed and sealed and John was duly removed from the line of succession. Sir Walter died soon afterwards and all his wealth passed onto his young wife and her brother.

However, the story did not end there. The news of the white hand soon spread about the nobility, and several friends of the disinherited heir spoke up in his favour. At Sir Walter's funeral the trustees of John's late mother arrived and put a halt to the ceremony at the church door and brought a claim against Lady Catherine. Eventually a compromise was agreed to; John Long inherited Wraxall, and Lady Catherine's son would gain Draycot. It was these events, so the story goes, that led to the two estates being divided. The Longs retained Wraxhall until 1805, when Sir James Tylney Long died without an heir.

Fairies of Hackpen Hill

Bronze Age barrows and burial mounds were once popularly believed to be fairy hills, and upon Hackpen Hill, near the village of Winterbourne Bassett, were two such mounds, although little (if anything) now remains of them owing to damage and quarrying over the years.

Fairies could be helpful little critters, but they had to be treated in just the right way, otherwise they would turn their wrath upon the person concerned. In many parts of rural England fairies could be encouraged by keeping a clean hearth and setting out a dish of clean water, milk and bread, and in return the fairies would churn cream and carry out other household chores during the night.

However, a more sinister side to the fairies was their habit of stealing young children and replacing them with one of their own offspring in disguise, to be raised by the human mother. These were known as Changelings, and in some cases young adults could also be taken by the fairies in such manner, either to force the human to marry a fairy wife or get a human mother to care for the fairy babies in their secret hidden world inside the fairy mounds.

It is this latter to which the fairies of Hackpen Hill are said to have had a liking for. Writing in the late seventeenth century, John Aubrey informs us that 'Some were led away by the Fairies, as was a Hind riding upon Hakpen with corne, led a dance to ye Devises. So was a shepherd of Mr Brown, of Winterburn-Basset.'

The Hackpen Fairies did not appear to imprison their human captives for long, however, since they were always returned, albeit in a different state; Aubrey tells us that the men were never able to enjoy themselves again upon coming back to the human world. The above-mentioned shepherd told Aubrey that 'ye ground opened, and he was brought into strange places underground, where they used musicall Instruments, viols, and Lutes'.

Hackpen Hill continues to be a hotspot for strange local phenomenon, including crop circles.

Hackpen Hill.
(Vieve Forward)

9

The Dart in the Tower

Approximately 40 to 50 feet up the south side of St Mary's Church tower at Calne, on the west-facing buttress, is an object that, while hard to see (unless you know what you are looking for), is not what you would expect to find stuck in the wall of a church. Several churches across the UK can claim to have cannonballs embedded in them (or once embedded in them), but Calne is a little different. Here, the church can claim to have a dart sticking out of its stonework.

The story of how this dart ended up in its unusual final resting place so far above the ground is one that has been related to me by an eyewitness.

It was during the 1970s that a bunch of men, after a hard day at work, decided to have a few drinks in the Butchers Arms in Church Street. It was also decided to have a friendly game of darts, and the drinks continued to flow as the game progressed. One of the men (who I will not name) lost the game and felt a bit put out; going outside he looked up at the church and threw the dart that he still held in his hand as hard as he could from the front door of the pub. It was quite some shot – the distance from pub to church tower is around 150 feet, and, as mentioned, the dart found itself lodged into solid stone some 40 to 50 feet above the ground. The yellow flight has long since disappeared, as has the plastic shaft, but the barrel still juts out of the buttress. However, after almost fifty years the tip is rusting, so be careful when walking along the churchyard path below the tower lest you be in for an unpleasant surprise!

Calne's church tower also has another interesting tale. The fabric of the building had been ignored for some time, as was not at all unusual in the decades prior to the English Civil War, and had fallen into a state of dangerous disrepair.

St Mary's Church, Calne.

Dart in the tower.

To compound matters further, the supporting pillars inside the tower had been too weak to bear the weight of masonry above them, having been built of hollow 'freestone' (a soft stone meant for decorative work) and in-filled with mortar and gravel, and so it was only a matter of time before disaster struck.

Finally, on 25 September 1638, the tower (belfry and all) collapsed, destroying parts of the chancel. In the following January, the town petitioned King Charles I for £3,000 to rebuild the church, claiming that aside from the tower, the chancel, three side chapels and the north and south transepts had also been destroyed. It seems that people were not above falsifying insurance claims even back then!

Repairs were soon undertaken and local tradition asserts that the famed architect Inigo Jones was brought in to survey the damage by a wealthy inhabitant of Calne at great personal expense, and that he designed the new tower that still stands. The works seems to have taken quite some time, since in 1650 the churchwardens were still spending out for repairs.

Former Butcher's Arms, Church Street.

Wild Will Darrel

The manor at Littlestone came into the Darrel family in 1415 with the marriage of William Darrel and Elizabeth Calstone. The original thirteenth-century house was replaced in the Tudor era by Sir George Darrell, whom we first met in a previous chapter, when his daughter married Sir Thomas Long.

Littlestone was passed along the Darrell line to Sir George's son, Edward, and then to his son, William, in 1549. It is to this William that the name of Wild Will is assigned.

The story (of which several versions exist) begins in the latter years of the sixteenth century. At this time, Mother Barnes was a well-known and highly respected midwife in the local area. On the night in question, she had just returned home from visiting a client in the late hours and had intended to spend what was left of the night asleep. However, no sooner had she shut her eyes than she was roused by a knock at the door. Mother Barnes desired to send her assistant, but the messenger was most insistent that she come in person. Finally giving in,

Littlecote House. (Steve Daniels)

Mother Barnes left her house and entered into the darkness of night, and this was the last that was seen of her for many hours to come.

The story of what happened during her disappearance was told by Mother Barnes in the presence of a magistrate, and such was the scandal that the matter was brought to trial.

Mother Barnes stated that as she unlocked the door and partly opened it, a hand forced its way through the gap, knocked the candle out of her hands and pulled her into the road outside. Mother Barnes lived in an isolated cottage, well away from any other sign of civilisation, and so as was the custom of the time, she desired to wear a hat to protect herself from the chilly air. The mysterious stranger refused, and instead told her to wrap a handkerchief over her head – there was another woman in great need of Mother Barnes' services and there was no time for delay. A horse was waiting close by, and Mother Barnes and the stranger mounted it before making a brisk trot through the countryside.

They had travelled almost a mile before Mother Barnes could not hold in her fear any longer and demanded to know the reason for the rude awakening. The man assured her that she was in no danger and would be handsomely paid later on. Around 2 miles further on the horse left the road and trotted through fields, across two rivers and through many a field gate. After an hour and a half they finally arrived at a paved courtyard in front of a great house. Mother Barnes was helped to alight from the horse and was taken through a long, narrow, dark passage into the house.

The stranger again informed Mother Barnes that no harm would come to her, and that she was to remain calm, but that he would have to blindfold her. Being in no position to refuse, the blindfold was applied and she was conducted into another room. Again, the stranger spoke up, informing her that they were now standing in the bedchamber with a lady in labour and that Mother Barnes was to carry out her duty, but was forbidden from removing her blindfold.

Mother Barnes claimed to be so paralysed with fear that she could not move for some time, but eventually a baby boy was safely delivered and placed into the care of a servant. The mother in question appeared to be a very young woman, but Mother Barnes dared not speak a word throughout the ordeal.

As soon as her work was complete, Mother Barnes was offered a glass of wine and told to prepare for the return home, which would be via a different, more lengthy route than the one used on the journey to the house. She asked to be seated in a chair while her horse was being readied, and in so doing pretended to fall asleep.

When sure that she would not be seen, she cut a small piece of material from the bed curtain and concealed it upon her person. She also made note of a strange burning smell that pervaded all the passages and hallways in the house as she was taken back outside into the courtyard.

The journey was long, but around 50 yards from her cottage the horse was brought to a halt and she was helped to dismount. The rider gave her a purse with twenty-five guineas and made her swear to secrecy. Finally, the blindfold was removed and Mother Barnes was let go.

When the sun came up, Mother Barnes went to see the magistrate and told him of the story. Using the material she had cut, and a description of her movements through the house, the magistrate deduced that she had been taken to Littlecote, the house of Wild Will Darrell, known for leading a debauched and depraved life. It was found that the strange burning smell had been caused by Wild Will tossing the newborn onto a fire and he was brought to trial at Salisbury on a charge of murder.

Darrell, however, escaped justice by bribing the judge (Sir John Popham), who afterwards became the new owner of Littlecote. While he may have escaped the law, he could not escape Fate, and soon afterwards Wild Will died a violent death after falling from his horse.

For a long time this story was held to be a work of pure fiction (for indeed some of the dates and timings do not match the records), but other documents came to light in the late nineteenth century, including Mother Barnes' testimony and a letter found at Longleat, that suggest that it may actually be true after all.

A Town Underground

Unlike during the Second World War there was no programme of providing public shelters during the Cold War when nuclear weapons threatened to set the world aflame. Instead, people were instructed to build a safe area in their homes, or to lie on the ground if caught outside. For the government, however, it was a different matter. Deep bunkers were constructed to safely house the politicians and civil servants in the event of war. Of these underground spaces one was built at Burlington Bunker at Corsham in the 1950s, and it was retained in this role until as recently as 2004.

The history of the site dates back much further, to around a century earlier when the caverns were excavated to mine stone. Later, in 1935, the former quarry was converted into an ammunition depot, and a railway was created to service the bunker, which totalled around 50 acres in size.

The tunnels remained in military hands during the Second World War, and the facilities were gradually improved. By 1943, part of the tunnel system had been

Railway entrance to Corsham Tunnels. (Elliott Simpson)

converted into an underground aircraft factory safe from the German bombers overhead, while the remainder continued to operate as the ammunition depot into the late 1960s.

In the previous decade, a section of the facility was fortified and strengthened into a nuclear bunker, code-named Burlington Bunker, capable of housing the prime minster and up to 4,000 civil servants to enable the government to remain functional should nuclear war break out. This marked the beginning of the site's use in such a capacity. The Burlington Bunker was designed to be completely self-sufficient so that it could operate in isolation, including an underground hospital, kitchen, fuel depots, underground water reservoir and accommodation. When the ammunition depot pulled out in the 1960s, Burlington Bunker became the main purpose of the site.

Of course, such war never did occur, and with the fall of the Iron Curtain and breakup of the Soviet Union in 1991, the bunker was stood down, but not mothballed. It was retained until 2004 in a state of readiness in case it should be needed once again in a hurry, but by this time the threat had passed and the costs of maintenance exceeded any useful purpose that the bunker could hold, and so the facility was decommissioned and its equipment and supplies removed.

Today, the site remains in MoD hands and the area has become the home of Information Systems & Services, a digital defence and communications hub, and parts of the tunnels have been leased out to private enterprises.

Unsurprisingly, a top-secret facility such as the Corsham Tunnels has attracted a slew of urban legends over the years, of which the most popular is that the tunnels held a fleet of steam trains that would have been brought out when all the diesel and electric trains had been destroyed or rendered useless by nuclear bombs. Alternatively, the tunnels were said to house 15,000 Jeeps for the same purpose. Another rumour holds that a still-secret tunnel was built connecting Burlington Bunker with the London Underground so that the government could escape the capital unseen in the event of war.

Britain's Area 51

Close to Corsham is Rudloe Manor. This former Royal Air Force base looks like any other manor house, set in a large garden surrounded by a low stone wall along a narrow country lane. An iron gate is set between two large stone pillars in the sweeping gateway, and beyond a long driveway stretches up to the house, providing extensive views out across the rolling Wiltshire countryside. At first glance all seems pretty much ordinary, except that it all kind of looks a bit neglected – the grass hasn't been mown for a while, the driveway has been consumed by weeds, and you get the sense that the house is empty.

However, like Corsham, Rudloe's real secret lies below ground, where an extensive underground city covers an estimated 2.2 million square feet of tunnels, bunkers and caverns. As at Corsham, Rudloe's life started out as a quarry for Bath stone, and was later taken over by the military in the lead-up to the Second World War, where the tunnels also formed an underground aircraft factory.

Unlike at Corsham, Rudloe has remained in military hands ever since, and it is the highly secretive nature of the site that has led to countless conspiracies and urban legends springing up. This is perhaps not so surprising when you consider that, up until 1992, Rudloe Manor was the central co-ordinating site for the Flying Complaints Flight, which was responsible for investigating reports of UFOs made by the various RAF stations scattered about the UK – a fact that was not made public by the MoD until 2010; until this time, there had been an active denial that the MoD were involved in investigating UFOs.

The theories as to Rudloe's involvement in secret alien technology came to the fore in 1955, when the American journalist Dorothy Kilgallen claimed that Britain had recovered a crashed UFO on 22 May and that scientists and airmen, 'after examining the wreckage ... are convinced that these strange aerial objects are not optical illusions or Soviet inventions, but actually are flying saucers which originate on another plant'. Kilgallen claimed that the news was fed to her by 'a British official of cabinet rank who prefers to remain unidentified'. This government source told Dorothy that the craft had been piloted by humanoid creatures, around 4 feet tall.

Almost immediately Rudloe Manor came under suspicion by the Ufologist community as the site where this alien spaceship was being held, and ever since there have been theories as to all kinds of experiments being undertaken in the underground passages on alien technology.

In truth, Rudloe was simply a sister site of the Burlington Bunker at Corsham, and shares a similar history.

Rudloe Manor. (Keith Daulby)

13

Avebury Circle

Surprisingly, there is relatively little folklore associated with Avebury, but what there is, is perhaps interesting enough to make up for the lack of origin myths and fantastical tales of witches, wizards, giant men or aliens (although more recently, some have put forward the theory that Avebury Circle was created by Martian visitors). However, some of the individual stones have their own stories to tell.

The entire complex is vast, said to be the largest in the world, but it has been much mutilated over the centuries by wilful vandalism and destruction or demolition for building material. Nonetheless, what remains is still very impressive and worth a visit.

At the north-western entrance to the circle is a large diamond-shaped stone that almost juts out into the road; this is the so-called Diamond Stone and is said to cross the road when the church clock strikes midnight. Its opposite number, at the far southern entrance, is another enormous square-shaped stone known as the Devil's Chair due to a hollow space large enough for someone to sit. In so doing directly above you is a chimney-like hole that passes through the top of the stone. Various legends exist about this stone, including that it was where young girls would traditionally go to make wishes on Beltane (presumably having something to do with the moonlight shining down through the chimney onto

Avebury. (Detmar Owen)

them). Smoke is also said to have been seen coming out of the 'chimney', and in such cases it is probably best to give this stone a wide berth – it signifies that the devil is present. As is common at many sites with devil folklore, he can apparently be summoned by running around the stone 100 times. Several other stones have similar associations: the Devil's Quoits, and the Devil's Brand-Irons for example.

Serpents or dragons are another association with Avebury, with several sources citing a serpent-like nature to the avenue of stones leading to the circle, and inside the church (which has been built just outside the circle) the font is carved with serpent motifs being vanquished by a bishop or saint.

There was also an old belief (although it is not clear if it was a genuinely held belief or merely a tale told to travellers) that the stones grew from the earth, and that is why there are so many and why they are so big.

The circle is also said to be a hotspot for paranormal activity, with multiple reports of ghostly figures and lights among the stones at night, as well as visions of ancient fairs and even of stones that no longer exist.

Avebury was also the setting for the 1977 children's fantasy-horror drama *Children of the Stones*, branded by those who remember it as one of the scariest programmes ever produced for children. In the series, Avebury stands in for the fictional village of Milbury, which has been built inside of an ancient stone circle. The village is trapped in a time rift, where everything plays out repeatedly in a grand cycle, dating back to when the stones were erected by druids.

Avebury font. (Immanuel Giel)

14

Silbury Hill

Just outside of Avebury Circle is Silbury Hill, the largest man-made mound in Europe. It is an impressive sight, rising 130 feet into the sky and covering an impressive 5.5 acres at its circular base. Some estimates calculate that it took 700 men ten years to build, although there is evidence that it has been enlarged in three or four phases of its development.

Like many barrows and mounds in Wiltshire and beyond, Silbury Hill is no stranger to legends of buried treasure. The most common legend says that the Celtic King Sil is buried within the hill (variously in golden armour, in a golden coffin, or sitting astride a golden horse), and that on some nights he can be seen riding around the hill with the moonlight glinting off his armour. The stories have been a big attraction to would-be treasure hunters, however, with the first recorded excavations being in 1776. Another large excavation took place in 1849, when an incredibly violent thunderstorm erupted overhead, the booms of the thunder being such that the entire hill quaked on the spot; the local villagers at Avebury were not surprised – they thought that the disturbance of the mound had caused the storm to occur.

Silbury Hill. (Steve Daniels)

Another common story is that it was created by the devil when he dumped a load of earth on the spot. Depending on who tells the story, he was either on his way to Marlborough, Devizes or Avebury to bury the respective town, but was stopped in his tracks by a priest, saint or old man and dropped his load at Silbury Hill instead. One favoured tale is that Marlborough and Devizes were bitter enemies, and the former managed to persuade the devil to bury the latter under a pile of earth. However, Devizes folk were smart and collected up all the old boots they could find, put them in a sack and sent a man out to search for the devil. They met at Silbury Hill and the devil asked how much further it was to Devizes. The old man replied that he had set out from that town three years ago, and the sack was full of all the boots he had worn out since; the devil became disheartened and dropped his cargo.

Aside from these stories, other legends include it being a major marker on a ley line, and the local area has been a hotspot for crop circles and UFO sightings.

Silbury Hill was also a popular spot to celebrate Palm Sunday, when local people would process up to the top and feast on fig cakes. Other hills in Wiltshire were also the location for fairs up until the early twentieth century.

15

The Devil's Den

Atop Fyfield Down is a large chambered tomb consisting of a huge capstone (which weighs as much as 17 tons) held aloft by three other stones 5 or 6 feet above the ground.

Many stories have developed about this prehistoric monument, including that if water is poured into one of the natural cup-shaped cavities on the capstone at midnight that it will have disappeared by morning, having been consumed by the devil or an imp. Alternatively, the devil himself is said to appear at the very stroke of midnight with eight white oxen and attempts to pull the structure down, but fails due to the stones being so large and the uprights buried so deeply that it cannot be budged. Another legend tells of a white rabbit with fiery red eyes that sits atop the structure and directs the devil on how to pull the stones down. A variation on this tale says that some farmers once tried to pull off the capstone with twelve white oxen, but that the harness immediately broke to pieces as soon as they had been attached to the stones.

The Devil's Den. (Mark Percy)

Stones on Fyfield Down. (Chris Andrews)

The stones were also used to warn local children to behave themselves; if a good little boy or girl walks around them, nothing will happen, but if a bad child circles the tomb seven times a toad will leap out and spit fire at them.

16

Oliver's Castle

Oliver's Castle was once originally called Roundway Camp or Roundway Castle, and is an Iron Age hillfort atop the Wiltshire Downs. However, in 1643 a major battle of the English Civil War was fought nearby between the Royalist forces of Lord Wilmot and the Parliamentarian army of Sir William Waller, and since then the site has gained the name of Oliver's Castle in the (false) belief that Oliver Cromwell himself had either built the fort here or otherwise occupied it.

Perhaps it is due to this fierce battle that the location has many ghost stories attached to it, for indeed despite vastly outnumbering their opponents, Waller's army lost an estimated 600 men killed and 1,200 captured, with countless others wounded. A headless ghost is said to once have stalked the hillside until a nearby barrow was excavated in 1855. There have also been countless reports of the sounds of battle heard on the hill, and of a large black dog that stalks the area.

Oliver's Castle. (Michael Dibb)

Jack Spratt's Clock

Up until 1911, St Andrew's Church at Wootton Rivers did not have a clock and some villagers thought that installing one would be a fitting way to mark the coronation of King George V. However, well intentions are one thing, but reality is quite another and the village simply could not afford to carry out such an endeavour.

This is when John Kingston Spratt, better known as Jack Spratt, stepped in to lend a hand. Jack had been born in the village in 1858 and spent his early life working on the local farms, but he had an inventive mind and taught himself the art of clock making. He offered to make the desired timepiece free of charge on condition that the villagers supplied him with all the scrap iron, lead, steel and brass as would be required.

Soon, Jack's cottage (now called Clock House) became the centre of the operation, and the garden was quickly buried under old agricultural machinery,

The Clock House. (Stuart Logan)

bicycles, bedsteads, fire irons, brass weights and all sorts of other scrap items. He began piecing together the various parts, including a pendulum made out of a broom handle and the bell hammer made out of a piece of a steam engine. The most delicate parts, of course, are the cogs, and Jack had hoped to employ the services of a London clock maker to make those items, but he did not receive a response. Instead, he knocked up some wooden samples and sent them to a local blacksmith to make out of metal.

Once the mechanism had been completed and installed, Jack made three clock faces to peer out of the church tower, each of which was an iron disc enamelled with white and numbered in black. Of these, one was particularly unique, since it does not have any numbers, but letters, which spell out the words GLORY. BE.TO.GOD. Despite being pieced together from scrap that had no business being a clock, it worked perfectly and was all up and running in time for the coronation.

However, Jack was not finished there. The following year, he produced a set of chimes to be added to the clock and, in his style, they were made from items of junk; the quarter-hour is marked with a different tune between the hours of twelve and six and the hour is sounded by the main bell.

The villagers voted their appreciation to Jack for his work, and after more than 110 years, the clock is still keeping time for the village.

Jack's clock. (Bill Royds)

A Long Way from Home

Approximately 41 miles south of Rowde is the churchyard of St Andrew's Church, Kinson, Dorset. Here, so far from Wiltshire, is a grave with the following epitaph:

To the memory of Robert Trotman, late of Rowd, in
the county of Wilts, who was barbarously murdered
on the shore near Poole, the 24th March, 1765.
A little tea, one leaf I did not steal,
For guiltless bloodshed I to God appeal;
Put tea in one scale, human blood in t'other
And think what 'tis to slay a harmless brother.

Above: St Andrew's Church, Kinson. (JBattersby)

Below: Kinson churchyard. (Lewis Clarke)

Robert Trotman was a Wiltshire smuggler, part of a gang that used the church at Kinson as a hiding place before carrying the contraband inland to Wiltshire; an old, empty altar tomb in the churchyard and a vault in the tower were the supposed hiding places. Perhaps seeing as though he lived just a couple of miles outside of Devizes, could Trotman be one of the original Moonrakers for whom the county nickname was created?

It was perhaps while collecting some of the illegal tea stored at Kinson, or maybe it was while unloading the goods from the boats shored up on the coast, that Trotman's gang encountered the excisemen. Since smuggling was a capital offence such encounters often got extremely violent as the gangs tried to escape with their lives; this case was no different. During the fight, Trotman was shot and killed, but such was the high regard that many people had for the smugglers that he was given a burial in the local churchyard and a headstone erected with the epitaph above, stating that he had been murdered by the king's men in the course of his work.

Rowde village.

19

The Seend Giant

Said to have been Britain's tallest man, if the statements as to his height are true then Frederick John Kempster – the Seend Giant – was (and remains) one of the tallest people who ever lived.

He was born in Bayswater, Westminster, in 1889 and came to live at the Barge Inn, Seend Cleeve, at the age of twenty-two. As the youngest of five children, his immense size is something of a mystery, since both his parents, and all of his siblings, were of average height. At the age of twenty-two, Frederick had shot up to 8 feet 2 inches and weighed 27 stone, and was still growing; he finally reached the height of 8 feet 4.5 inches by the time he died in 1918, at the young age of twenty-nine.

When a local newspaper wrote a report about him in 1916, Frederick had already become a celebrity, having been touring around England and appearing at fairs and exhibitions as a means of earning a living. The article explained how he travelled in the guard's carriage when on tour by train, because a normal passenger cabin could not hold him, and that his lodgings consisted of three beds pushed together. 'He can comfortably light a cigarette at a street lamp,' the article continued, 'and can span two octaves on the keyboard of a pianoforte. A penny will pass through his signet ring, and his size in boots is 22½.'

Frederick's demise began when, having been touring in Germany in 1914, the First World War broke out. He was arrested and interned and fell ill during his two years as a prisoner of war before negotiations resulted in his release. Returning to Wiltshire, his health never recovered, although he still went on tour. It was while in Blackburn in 1918 that he contracted the pneumonia that killed him in April of that same year. He was buried in Blackburn Cemetery.

Barge Inn, Seend Cleeve. (Rodw)

The Devizes Wizard

During the reign of James I lived a man known as Cantelow, who was a fortune-teller and general Wise Man of Devizes. The story that concerns us took place at the very end of the king's reign, when the vicarage house of Wilcot became embroiled in a deep and dark mystery involving the ceaseless tolling of one of the church bells. Stranger still was that the sound was entirely confined to those inside the vicarage; it is said that a person had to be within the house itself to hear the bell, and that even by poking your head out of a window the sound would disappear.

The ghostly audible apparition became a novelty for the local gentry, who found great pleasure in visiting Wilcot to the great annoyance of the lord of the manor, Sir George Wroughton. Even the king himself is alleged to have sent down a gentleman of his court to investigate the matter.

Many years later, in 1705, Sir George's elderly son, Francis Wroughton, wrote down an account of how the events began despite being away at school at the time. He explained how, on one late evening, a 'debauched person' arrived at the vicarage and demanded the keys to the church tower so that he could ring the bells himself. The vicar, William Palmer, refused on account of the lateness of the evening and that it would inconvenience Sir George in the adjoining manor house.

Cantelow, the Devizes Wizard (*A History of the Ancient Borough of the Devizes*).

Embarrassed and put out, the stranger departed, but vowed to himself that he would get revenge upon the vicar. Unsure how to go about this, he went to the Devizes Wizard to seek his aid. The wizard declared that the vicar shall be plagued by the bells, and from that moment on the paranormal ringing of the bell in the vicarage commenced.

After the king's man had returned and reported the strange events, the king had Cantelow thrown into Fisherton Gaol for the rest of his life, and the wizard avowed that the tolling of the bell will not cease until he was dead. Soon afterwards, the king died, and Cantelow gained his freedom; it appears that the ringing at Wilcot also ceased at the same time.

Right: Wilcot Church tower and belfry.

Below: Wilcot Manor.

A Death in the Market Place

A panel on the east side of the Market Cross at Devizes carries a rather interesting inscription:

On Thursday the 25th of January 1753, Ruth Pierce of Potterne in the County agreed with three other women to buy a sack of wheat in the market, each paying her due proportion towards the same. One of these women, in collecting the several quotas of money, discovered a deficiency, and demanded of Ruth Pierce the sum which was wanting to make good the amount. Ruth Pierce protested that she had paid her share, and said, 'She wished she might drop down dead if she had not.' She rashly repeated this awful wish; when, to the consternation and terror of the surrounding multitude, she instantly fell down and expired, having the money concealed in her hand.

Above: Plaque on the Market Cross. (Matt Brown)

Left: Devizes Market Cross.

Originally, a tablet with this warning was displayed in the old market house, but when this building was demolished a landlord of the Bear Inn had it inscribed on a pair of pillars at the Market Cross. This, too, was removed in 1801. However, a few years later Lord Sidmouth had the present cross erected and the mayor ordered that the inscription be added onto one of the panels as a warning to all future generations against 'invoking the Sacred Name, to conceal the devices of fraud and falsehood'. It is more likely, however, that poor Ruth died of a heart attack brought on by the stress of being accused, but the truth has never got in the way of a bit of moralising.

This is not the first time that the Market Place was scene of an untimely death with a religious aspect to it. In around 1523, John Bent, a tailor of Urchfont, was burnt at the stake there on a charge of a denial of the Holy Sacrament.

There is also another monument in the town erected as a warning against ignoring Church doctrine. This is a tall obelisk within St John's churchyard that serves as the grave of five men who, on a Sunday in 1751, drowned in Drews Pond after deciding to sail on the water. Unfortunately, they did not have a boat and so used a cooler instead. The obelisk bears the warning 'Remember the Sabbath day, to keep it holy'.

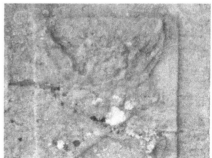

Above left: Memorial to the drowned sailors.

Top right: The obelisk's warning inscription is now almost lost.

Above right: Skull and crossbones on the Devizes obelisk.

22

Medieval Monsters, Ecclesiastical Exhibitionists

St John the Baptist's Church in Devizes has a long and particularly fascinating history, but it wasn't until 2006 that an unusual carving was 'discovered' on the church. The image inscribed into the stonework, although badly eroded, graphically depicts the figure of a Sheela-na-gig.

Such carvings are not uncommon in the British Isles (and across parts of Europe), but what business do such graphically sexual figures (usually of naked women with exaggerated 'features') have in medieval Christian churches? Particularly when they date back to a time when lust, sexuality and the female form were considered sinful?

Various theories have been put forward as to the meaning of these symbols, from a hang-over of Pagan fertility goddesses and beliefs, to warnings against the sins of lust and carnal desire. Simon Brighton suggests that the symbolism of the Sheela-na-gigs dates back to as early as 445 BC, and that in the ancient Celtic tradition the female form was traditionally associated with luck, peace and resolution of quarrels. Indeed, Hadrian's Wall still bears no fewer than fifty-nine carvings of male genitalia upon its stones as symbols of power and protection against the northern tribes. In this manner, it is supposed that Sheela-na-gigs offer a similar metaphysical warding-off power to protect the churches that bear them – similar to other more traditional gargoyles and grotesques that adorn many medieval churches.

The Devizes Sheela-na-gig (left).

Furthermore, Dr Oakley and Dr Woodcock (the 'discoverers' of the Devizes Sheela-na-gig) point out that St John's Church, being originally contained within the castle grounds and possibly erected on the orders of a secular patron, would not have been the most prudent location to display images supposedly serving as a warning to lustful women, especially when St Mary's Church (which does not have any such carvings) was more accessible to the medieval townsfolk. They suggest that this may lend evidence to the Devizes Sheela-na-gig being something that held a much greater meaning than as a mere warning against sin – that it was deliberately chosen to adorn the church perhaps as a status symbol.

The Sheela-na-gig at Devizes is not only special due to the fact that relatively few of these carvings still survive in their original location (only around eighty in Britain and Ireland), but also because it is one of only two or three in the UK that features an exhibitionist pair – a male and female. Despite being badly eroded, much detail still remains and shows both figures manipulating their greatly exaggerated genitalia with their hands.

These carvings still retain much emotion and power today, particularly for those ignorant of their historical and symbolic importance and meaning. It was only in 2004 that a Sheela-na-gig at Buncton in West Sussex (the only such example found in Sussex) was destroyed with a hammer and chisel in a late-night act of vandalism. Indeed, the very act of the destruction of this centuries-old carving brought out strong arguments on both sides, with some parishioners glad that the 'pagan' symbol was destroyed.

Elsewhere on the church can be found other grotesques performing various feats, including an animalistic monster pulling its hind legs up behind its ears to expose its anus to passersby, a monster devouring a sinner (said sinner's legs are all that are left, protruding out of the beast's cavernous mouth), and another pair in which a monstrous animal and a human are joined at the mouths with a piece of rope while the human figure appears to be holding his/her (it is very eroded) genitals with their free hand. Near to the Sheela-na-gig pair is also a carving depicting another male-female couple embracing each other inside the mouth of a bestial creature.

Above left: Copulating couple being devoured (right) and figures joined at the mouth (left).

Above right: A monster eats a sinner (centre).

23

Siege of Devizes

During the early years of the English Civil War, Devizes found itself in a tricky position. Politically, the town was Parliamentarian, but the local civil leadership were staunch Royalists. Geographically, Devizes was directly in the line of fire between the king's headquarters at Oxford and the Royalist strongholds in the south-west. Almost immediately upon outbreak of hostilities Parliament had control of almost all ports along the English coast, giving them a distinct advantage in both supplying their own armies, but also blocking overseas reinforcements and supplies to the king's forces. Charles I had recruited vast numbers of men in Ireland, but needed a place where they could be brought in; Bristol was the ideal solution. Wiltshire, in the first half of 1643, now found itself the key battleground between the opposing factions, with each attempting to force the other out of the south-west.

Devizes was immediately put on a war footing when the king raised his Royal Standard at Nottingham on 22 August 1642, effectively serving as his declaration of war against parliament. By July 1643 the town was in Royalist hands.

Earlier in the year, the Parliamentarian army (under Sir William Waller) and the Royalist army (under Sir Ralph Hopton) began a series of clashes across Somerset and north Wiltshire as Waller attempted to cut off the king's advance to Bristol. In March, Waller had advanced from his successes in Sussex into Wiltshire,

'Waller Storms Devizes, July 1643' (*A History of the Ancient Borough of the Devizes*).

passing though Salisbury and then into the northern parts of the county. On the 22nd, he succeeded in taking Malmesbury and then made a night-time crossing of the River Severn to take Gloucester by surprise, capturing the entire Royalist garrison. From here, he had further successes at Hereford and Tewkesbury before turning south and marching upon Bath. Here, he encountered Prince Maurice, Lord Hopton and Sir Bevill Granville as they headed north from raising forces in Devon and Cornwall. Among the Royalist armies were many of the Wiltshire gentry, and battle was given at Lansdowne Hill on 5 July 1643.

The result was inconclusive; at best a pyrrhic victory for Lord Hopton – Waller retreated back to Bath, but the Royalists had lost most of their cavalry, ammunition and three commanders wounded or killed; Lord Hopton himself was also injured in an explosion. Whereas Waller had cleverly left a garrison to defend Bath from which he could replace those lost in the battle, the only means of repair for Hopton's army was in pushing with all due haste for Oxford. As a result, the Royalist army marched to Chippenham on 8 July and thence to Devizes on the 9th, where a small ammunition store had been arranged. So began the four-day Siege of Devizes.

Small bodies of Waller's men kept up a running skirmish with Hopton's rearguard all the way from Chippenham to Devizes, but failed to intercept the main bulk of the army before they reached the safety of the town. On the night of the 9th, Waller set up camp near Rowde, and early the next morning sent 5,500 men to skirt the town and cut off a potential Royalist retreat to Marlborough. He also sent a scouting party out on the 11th to find the Royalist supply wagon that was en route to Devizes. The supply party was discovered at

The siege as depicted on Devizes'
Millennium Cross.

Devizes Castle gatehouse.

Beckhampton and after a short skirmish, Waller's men returned with 200 Royalist prisoners and five wagons of ammunition.

Meanwhile, the Royalists were not idle; their artillery was set up in the remains of the castle, the roads were blocked and barricaded, and the infantry dispersed around the town. St John's Church was also requisitioned as a gunpowder store.

Waller opened the siege proper on 11 July, keeping up a near-continuous artillery bombardment on the town and castle throughout the day and into the next. With the defences softened, he then sent his infantry to take the town, with vicious hand-to-hand fighting spreading throughout the streets. Small artillery loaded with solid shot and grapeshot were also brought in, and traces of the battle can still be seen in scars at both St John's and St James's Churches.

Civil War damage at St John's Church.

Civil War damage is also visible on St James' Church tower.

On the 12th, with parts of the town in ruin and the fighting still running through the streets, 1,500 cavalry had been sent out from Oxford to reinforce Hopton's besieged men. On the route this force was reinforced by other troops, two artillery pieces and ammunition wagons before reaching Marlborough. In Devizes, and despite being outnumbered and poorly equipped, Hopton's men managed to regroup and repulse Waller's army. The two forces would come to face each other again the following day upon Roundway Down, near to Oliver's Castle.

As a result of the siege, legends of hauntings at Devizes Castle exist. One ghost is said to be that of a Royalist soldier seen running up and down the main staircase with his sword. Reports of encounters with the ghost say that an icy chill is left in the spectre's wake as he brushes past the witness.

The Devizes Pyramid, depicting the castle in its heyday.

The Truth Will Out

When a farmer was murdered and robbed at Pewsey in 1798, the crime may have gone unsolved if it wasn't for the clever detective work of the local vicar – or so legend would have us believe.

The tale begins when a local farmer took refreshment at the Phoenix Inn after the market had ended. Becoming boastful after enjoying his libations a little too much, he showed the other patrons all the coins he had earned selling his livestock. Naturally, such boasting brought out the envy in some of the patrons, and when the farmer departed, he never arrived at his destination and was reported missing. His body was later found on the road from Pewsey, devoid of all the coins.

It was evident that someone from the bar had been responsible for the murder, but suspects were many and evidence was scarce. The vicar, Joseph Townsend, was aware of an old superstition that a murdered man's corpse will be able to identify his killer when in his presence, much like the belief that a murder victim's final moment would be 'burned' into the retinas of his eyes.

The vicar had the farmer's body brought into the church and laid out. He then ordered everyone in the village to parade into the church, place his (or her) hand

Former Phoenix Inn. (Chris Talbot)

upon the dead man's face and swear as to his innocence. Person after person filed through the church to conduct this morbid charade, until one man by the name of Amor was called up to take his turn. Amor became very nervous and afraid and refused to carry out the test. Clearly he was the guilty party, and he was immediately arrested, tried and hanged in 1799 … except this tale is entirely a work of fiction, since there is no record of Revd Townsend conducting such a test, and there is no record of a man named Amor being hanged – in fact there were no executions for murder in Wiltshire at all in 1798 or 1799.

Nonetheless, Revd Townsend was an unorthodox and controversial character in real life, for he truly was the vicar of Pewsey. However, his actual 'claim to fame' was not solving an otherwise unsolvable murder, but for his treatise abhorring the idea of helping the poor. Giving assistance to the poor, whether inside or outside of the workhouse, only served to allow the propagation of the 'weak' at the expense of the 'strong', and instead he advocated abolishing all aid to the poor. As someone who was clearly a follower of the concept of the 'undeserving poor' (i.e. that a person was poor only because he was lazy and unwilling to work), he considered that people should be left to starve until they are so incentivised to seek work. 'Hunger,' he said, 'will tame the fiercest animals, it will teach decency and civility, obedience and subjugation to the most brutish, the most obstinate, and the most perverse'.

St John the Baptist's Church, Pewsey. (Richard Humphrey)

The Urchfont Killer

Aside from Pewsey, a former pub at Urchfont laid claim to its own legend of murder – said to be the first serial killings in the whole of Wiltshire. For some time in the late eighteenth and early nineteenth centuries, there was a small inn at Lydeway called The Shepherd and Dog owned by Thomas Burry.

Burry soon gained a reputation for himself as rumours spread that lonely travellers had been seen going into the pub, but never coming out again. Despite these rumours it would seem that no one ever thought to investigate or report the matter to the appropriate authorities, since Burry was able to continue his trade until he died in 1842. The story goes that he was never tried or convicted for any murders, but that after his death the back garden of the pub was dug up and twelve bodies were exhumed – men that had been robbed and killed by the evil landlord.

Unlike his supposed victims, Burry was afforded a funeral and decent burial, but it is said that the church bellringers refused to carry out their duty at the service.

Above: Lydeway, Urchfont.

Left: St Michael and All Angels, Urchfont. (Tim Heaton)

The Secret of the Sheep Stealer

On 14 December 1661 a letter from John Hoskins, a sergeant-at-law in London, to the Wiltshire historian John Aubrey asked about a story that had come to his attention regarding the village of Steeple Ashton. In 1620, John Brewer was indicted in the village for sheep stealing and was alleged to be able to keep the meat fresh and unspoiled for as long as seven weeks without the need for salting or other means of preservation. At the trial, the judge wished to know John's secret, but his lips remained sealed. John was eventually acquitted through lack of evidence, and now, forty years later, John Hoskins desired to know how Brewer kept the meat for so long. After all, in 1661 meat was still expensive and even for those that could afford it the real trouble was how to store it safely during the hot summer months. In short, Hoskins wanted Aubrey to find out 'how to keep mutton sweet for seven weeks without salt'.

Aubrey's investigations were short, and his response even shorter: 'Near Claverton, by Bath, in the stone quarries, are some caves; and this Brewer the sheepstealer kept his stolen sheep in the caves, alive! This was the secret.'

Cave at Claverton. (Neil Owen)

The Black Dog

Near to Collingbourne Kingston lies the expanse of Collingbourne Wood in which a large black dog, with large, glowing yellow eyes, had a taste for people of ill intent and evil hearts.

The origin of this story dates back to the seventeenth or eighteenth century when a pair of highway robbers made a habit of terrorising travellers along the Bath road, stealing whatever they could from whomever they could – no one was spared. However, the men did not only target the highway, but also burgled houses too. It was on one of these 'jobs' that the men were disturbed and killed the old farmer and his wife, then set fire to the house to cover their tracks.

This was the final straw for the people of Collingbourne Kingston, and they set out to find the murderers. The men were found one dark night and were chased through nearby Everleigh until they were able to escape into Collingbourne Wood. Thinking they were safe, they hadn't reckoned with the canine protector and his hatred of wrongdoers of every kind, and what worse than a double murder? The pursuers refused to enter the wood, but the two men headed deeper and deeper into the trees, attempting to get away from the shouting and hollering of the villagers.

However, as they went further into the woods, they saw a pair of great yellow eyes appear before them. In panic, the men fled back the way they came and ran straight into the arms of their pursuers. Securely restrained, the men were marched to Devizes and hanged.

The black dog of Collingbourne Kingston is still said to haunt the woods, and so you better be sure to avoid venturing too near it at night lest you have something on your conscience!

Collingbourne Wood. (Forester2009)

Cley Hill

Cley Hill, near Corsley, is another of those locations for which legends of the devil have developed. As with some of the stories of Silbury Hill, it seems that the poor folks of Devizes were again to be on the receiving end and the devil collected a large mound of earth with which to bury the town. However, as he crossed into Wiltshire from Somerset, he came across an old man and asked him how much further to Devizes. The old man replied that he didn't know – his beard had turned grey since he set out to find the town. As at Silbury Hill, the devil became disheartened at the thought of lugging such a heavy load much longer and dumped it to form Cley Hill.

A barrow atop Cley Hill was also once the home of the spiritual guardian of Bugley. A spring of water suddenly appeared under the hill one day, and the spirit, upon hearing the running water, used his powers to redirect its underground course so that it reached the surface at Hogs Well in the village. The spirit warned the people never to drink the water, but use it only to cure eye disorders. That night, an old woman ignored the warning and drank the water, only to die that same night. It was also said that a cow that had polluted the water met with an unfortunate end soon afterwards by drowning in the mud. The healing properties

Cley Hill. (David Howard)

of the water at Bugley was sought after until the early twentieth century, when bottles of it were still being sold for 6d.

The location of the hill so close to the Wiltshire-Somerset border is also another major reason why the site is steeped in folklore. One story that highlighted the rivalry between the two counties was that Cley Hill was kicked up by generations of Wiltshire folk having to wipe their dirty feet before being allowed to cross into the 'favoured soil' of Somerset! Alternatively, the hill was said to be a marker on the border between Warminster and Corsley, and as a result it was the custom for all differences to be put aside until Palm Sunday, when the two communities would gather on Cley Hill to fight it out. A Palm Sunday fair, known as the Bugley Fair, did indeed take place on Cley Hill for many years and was banned sometime in the late nineteenth century a result of the riotous behaviour that such merry meetings would bring forth.

Similarly, a Palm Sunday gathering was an annual event at Cow Down, near Longbridge Deverill, when boys would play a peculiar ball game on the hill. The boys would line up from the base of the hill all the way to the top, each armed with a stick. The boy at the bottom would hit a ball up to the next, and he in turn would hit it up to the next before it had chance to roll down again. This was continued until the ball got all the way to the top of the hill, and then the game was restarted over again.

Cow Down. (Maurice Pullin)

The Giant's Dance

Stonehenge is perhaps the most famous landmark in Wiltshire, and is perhaps one of the best-known ancient sites in the world. It would, therefore, be remiss not to explore some of the legends and folklore of these stones.

Many, many theories have been put forward to explain either the presence of Stonehenge or its purpose – some credible, others a little far-fetched. One story, by that most famous of Arthurian writers Geoffrey of Monmouth, is that of the Giant's Dance. In this tale, set in the tumultuous years at the end of the Roman era when the Saxons were invading southern England, the British and Saxon warlords met upon Salisbury Plain to give battle. On the one side was King Arthur and on the other was the great Saxon chieftain Hengist. King Arthur claimed another great victory against the Saxons and desired to commemorate the battle. Upon consulting Merlin, he was informed of a stone circle in Ireland known as the Giant's Dance that would be a fitting tribute to the British victory. Arthur agreed and went at once to Mount Killarney to steal the Giant's Dance, and on so doing it was brought back and erected upon Salisbury Plain. Indeed, the ancient name for Stonehenge was *choir-gaur*, meaning roughly 'dance of giants'. An alternative name was *stanhen gist*, meaning 'gallows stones'. Other builders of the circle include ancient Atlanteans and extraterrestrial visitors.

It was also said that it was impossible to count all the stones at Stonehenge, but if someone did manage to do so, they would die soon afterwards. Alternatively, in the early eighteenth century local children were told that the only way to count the stones was to place a loaf of bread at each one, otherwise the counter would certainly either miss a stone or count the same one twice.

The stones, being the fulcrum of multiple ley lines, are reputed to have many healing powers, and water charged in the circle could heal any condition.

Stonehenge from above, 1983. (Serendigity)

St Melor

The Breton saint St Melor has a long association with Amesbury, with the former abbey being his major shrine, and the present Church of St Mary and St Melor still bears his name.

A cult developed in his honour in tenth-century Brittany, where he was said to have been a prince until his father was murdered by his uncle. The uncle also desired to slay Melor so that there were no other claimants to the throne, but instead only cut off Melor's right hand and left foot. The young boy was then sent to Quimper Abbey to be raised, and it was here that he had a silver hand and a bronze foot surgically attached to his missing appendages.

As a devout Christian and deeply holy boy, the metal prostheses began to come alive as if they were really a part of his body, and also grew as he got older. Clearly, Melor was still a threat to his uncle's throne and so the boy was ordered to be murdered. A monk carried out the order and removed Melor's head, and the body was buried.

Later, Melor was sainted and his remains exhumed and taken to England. Upon reaching Amesbury Abbey the body was laid out on the altar and could not be moved, and so he was buried there. The Breton cult soon took hold in south-west England, and a later tradition developed that put St Melor as the son of a murdered Cornish duke.

St Mary and St Melor's Church. (Peter Trimming)

The Boscombe Down Incident

On 26 September 1994, a top-secret American stealth aircraft – far more advanced than anything ever flown to date – is alleged to have crashed at Boscombe Down late at night. The wreckage was quickly covered over and the Special Forces brought in to put the entire base – and surrounding area – on lock-down. The name of this aircraft was Project Aurora.

Project Aurora is said to have been a hypersonic spy plane built as a 'Black Project' at Area 51, and is meant to have been responsible for many sightings of strange, triangle-shaped aircraft and mysterious sonic booms during the 1980s and early 1990s. Naturally, all knowledge of the Aurora has been denied by governments for decades – so we are led to believe.

Boscombe Down. (M. J. Richardson)

In 1997, the respected *Air Forces Monthly* magazine reported the story of the incident in 1994, claiming that the Aurora crashed during takeoff. An unnamed eyewitness observed the wreckage being first covered with a tarpaulin and then removed to the corner of a secret hangar after the SAS were brought in to help with the clean-up. A few days later a C-5 transport aircraft was brought in and the wreckage was loaded aboard to be flown back to the USA.

Strange radio interceptions and sonic booms were reported from the USA, Netherlands and North Sea in the few years before and after the supposed crash at Boscombe Down, with the aircraft supposedly having been based at RAF Machrihanish, in north-west Scotland, for several years before being flown down to Wiltshire.

The incident, it is said, was covered up and all knowledge of the crash denied by the government consistently since 1994. Boscombe Down has continued to be the centre of conspiracy theories regarding exotic aircraft and alien technology on account of its role as a test site for experimental aircraft and proximity to Porton Down.

Leper Colony

The village of Maiden Bradley was once Wiltshire's leper colony. A hospital had been established there at some time before 1164 for wealthy maidens afflicted with the disease, and it later also became a priory. The hospital part of the priory closed down by around 1270 as the scale of leprosy in England had declined significantly by that point, but the priory continued until it was dissolved in 1536.

The history of the priory was fairly unremarkable, except for during the reign of the final prior, Richard Jennings (1506–36). Jennings claimed to have a papal licence that allowed him to break his vows of chastity and keep mistresses. As a result he developed a taste for pretty young women and

Site of Maiden Bradley Priory and leper hospital. (James Harrison)

took them into his private quarters. However, when they fell pregnant the prior would marry them off to other men and, it is said, he fathered multiple illegitimate children in this way.

There is also a legend regarding a plague colony at Fosbury Camp, near to the village that bears its name close to the Hampshire border. Similar to the plot of John Carpenter's 1980 horror film *The Fog*, when the plague reached the area in the 1660s, the rector of Vernham Dene (just across the border in Hampshire) persuaded all those with symptoms to leave the village and form a colony at Fosbury Camp (some versions say in Hippenscombe) safely away from the healthy. Convinced that they would be cared for and supplied with food and water, the plague victims were betrayed by the rector and left to starve to death. Contrary to the film's storyline, it is not the murdered victims that are said to haunt the hill, but the ghost of the rector, who wanders around the former camp seeking forgiveness for what he did.

Fosbury Camp. (Ian Freeman)

Egbert's Stones

Within the rectory garden at Kingston Deverill is a pair of large Sarsen stones standing upright at an angle so that their tops come together to form an upright triangle. These are said to be Egbert's Stones and were brought here from their original location on King's Court Hill, where there would have originally been a third stone to create an ancient chambered tomb.

Legend states that it was at Egbert's Stones (the original site) where King Alfred assembled the armies of Somerset, Hampshire and Wiltshire to march against the invading Viking hoards in AD 878. There had, prior to this point, been an uneasy truce between the two forces, but the Vikings broke the truce at Chippenham and caused King Alfred to flee south.

With his militia forces now assembled, King Alfred marched his men to meet the Vikings in battle at Edington, where the king gained a tremendous victory and ensured the survival of the West Saxons in southern England.

There are two other sites that lay claim to being the Egbert Stones – at Bourton and at King Alfred's Tower, all within close proximity to Kingston Deverill, although with the original location being atop a hill offering a panoramic view over the countryside, it is likely that it was here that the real meeting place of King Alfred's army was.

Above left: Egbert's Stones. (John Potts)

Above right: Stones at Bourton. (Michael Dibb)

The Maid and the Maggot

In Little Langford is a traditional folk story that a young maid was out collecting nuts in Grovely Wood when she came across one that contained a maggot. Instead of discarding the rotten nut, the maid kept it and took the maggot home as a pet, feeding and caring for it. The maggot grew larger and larger as each day passed, until one day it had become so large that it rose up and killed the maid.

Even up until the late eighteenth century, the villagers of Little Langford are said to have been so sure of the historical accuracy of the tale that the story had been carved into the church porch, and would point it out to passers-by. However, the carving actually depicts a boar hunt, complete with huntsmen and dogs, rather than a monstrous maggot, so it is also somewhat of a mystery why it was thought that the carving was assigned its traditional interpretation.

Above left: Grovely Wood. (Derek Harper)

Above right: Carving at Little Langford. (*Salisbury Plain*)

Oak Apple Day

Grovely Wood seems to be a magnet for traditions and folklore in that part of Wiltshire, and one that still occurs today is the custom of Oak Apple Day at Great Wishford on 29 May. On this day, a great festival takes place in which the villagers assert their lawful right to use Grovely Wood, beginning with the men cutting an oak bough from the wood in the early morning, which is then taken to the church, decorated with ribbons and displayed in front of the tower.

A group of women then dress in traditional costume and head to Salisbury Cathedral with bundles of wood and perform a special dance in The Close in honour of the women that protested against a former Lord of Wilton Manor who tried to stop the villagers from having access to the woods. Afterwards, a service is held inside the cathedral, where the ladies shout 'Grovely, Grovely and all Groveley' to claim their rights to the woods for another year. With this complete, they return to Great Wishford, where a village fair continues the celebration throughout the day.

Above: Collecting the boughs at Great Wishford. (*Salisbury Plain*)

Left: Grovely Wood. (Derek.hill)

36

The Bristol Cross

Within the grounds of Stourhead is the former Bristol Cross. This sculpture dates to the fifteenth or sixteenth century and is said to have been erected to mark the granting of the city's charter, and once stood at the crossroads of four major thoroughfares in the centre of Bristol. In 1733, the citizenry petitioned for its removal as a 'ruinous and superstitious relick'. As a result, the cross was dismantled and spent the next thirty years being moved around the city in various states of repair, until 1764 when the Bristol banker Henry Hoare acquired it and had it removed in half-a-dozen wagons to Stourhead, where he had it rebuilt. This is why the medieval Bristol Cross now stands in Wiltshire.

The Bristol Cross. (Odd Wellies)

The Four Sisters of Grovely Wood

Another legend of Grovely Wood tells the story of the four Hansel sisters. These Danish girls had moved to Wilton in 1737 at the same time as a smallpox outbreak left 132 people dead. The local villagers believed that the sisters were responsible for bringing the pestilence and accused them of witchcraft. They were apprehended and taken deep into Grovely Wood, where they were each bludgeoned to death and buried in four separate graves, each an appropriate distance from the other, so that they would be unable to use their dark powers, even in death, to plot more evil deeds.

Later, four beech trees mysteriously grew on the sites of the graves to mock the villagers for their crimes. The ghosts of the sisters are said to still haunt the woods, and many sightings have been reported. At the rear of one of the trees is a hollow cavity in which people still leave offerings to this day.

The woods are also said to have another ghost in the form of the Burcombe Woodsman – a poacher who was given a similar form of summary 'justice' by the locals and was hanged from a tree (another version says that the ghost was a man accidentally shot by a hunter).

Four Sisters, Grovely Wood.
(Derek Harper)

The Old Church of Old Sarum

Within the ancient hillfort of Old Sarum are the ruins of a cathedral, the footings of which can still be traced on the ground. John Aubrey wrote in the early eighteenth century of the story of how the church came to be demolished. It would seem that there were two problems with the location of the church. Firstly, it was built so high up, Aubrey said, that when the strong winds blew the worshippers could not hear the priest say Mass. Secondly, a fort was not the most convenient of places for a great cathedral to have been erected, and the priests and soldiers were always at odds with each other. The uneasy relationship continued until one day, when the priests had all left the church to attend the castle, the soldiers blocked their return and refused them entry into the church. The bishop went to the Lady Abbess at Wilton to see if another piece of land could be found on which to erect a new cathedral where the priests could live in peace.

The bishop and the abbess could not agree, despite many meetings over several days. However, when the bishop was asleep one night he had a dream in which Mary told him to build his new church on a plot of land at Merrifield, and this is how the current cathedral and city of Salisbury was formed.

Old Sarum from the air, 1983. (Serendigity)

Old Sarum Cathedral ruins. (Michael Dibb)

An alternative origin story for Salisbury is that an archer at Old Sarum couldn't decide where the new city should be built and so fired an arrow into the valley below the fort, and where it landed was where the new cathedral was built – some 2 miles away!

Salisbury from Old Sarum. (Roy Hastings)

39

Died before He Was Born

Within Salisbury Cathedral is a small blue tomb slab with the following curious epitaph:

> H S E – The body of Tho the sonn of Tho. Lambert gent. who was borne May ye 13 An Do 1683 & dyed Feb. 19 the same year.

How could this poor infant have died three months before he was even born? The answer is that in 1683, Britain was still using the old-style Julian calendar, which had New Year's Day on 25 March. This meant that the calendar year ran from March of one year to March of the other. Therefore, in the current Gregorian calendar, Thomas Lambert's date of birth would now be written as 13 May 1683, and his date of death as 19 February 1684; he died at the age of nine months, rather than three months before birth as first impression would have us believe.

Salisbury Cathedral. (Pualhaberstroh)

40

The Election Song

Upon election night in the Salisbury City Constituency, is has long been the tradition that the winning candidate sings the traditional Wiltshire song '*The vly be on the turmut*' from the balcony of the White Hart Hotel. This county tune about the trouble of keeping flies off the turnip crops became the marching song of the Wiltshire Regiment and, for some reason, eventually became tradition at election night for the past three centuries. The current Member of Parliament for the city (as at the time of writing) has kept up the tradition on the occurrence of his election and re-election since 2010.

White Hart Hotel balcony, Salisbury. (Jim Osley)

A Modern Monolith

Wiltshire is renowned for its multiple prehistoric stone circles and standing stones, but on 1 January 2021, the people of Salisbury woke up on a cold, frosty morning to find that an 8-foot-tall metal monolith had appeared on Laverstock Down. The object had a triangular cross-section and all three faces were polished to a mirror shine. The base of it had been buried into the hard ground, although there was little sign of any disturbance to the soil around it.

Similar objects have mysteriously appeared in dozens of places across the world during the previous year, including at Glastonbury Tor, Belgium, California, Romania and Ireland.

There have been no explanations yet given as to the meaning behind these sculptures, with some saying that they are extraterrestrial in nature, while most understand them to be man-made. Maybe the purpose or reason for these mystical monuments will be explained one day, or like all good mysteries, the truth will never really be known.

Laverstock Down. (David Martin)

Moonrakers,
Dabchicks and Gudgeons

There are many nicknames for the good folk of Wiltshire. Chief among them are the Moonrakers – a general term for any native of the county. This term has often been used as a means of offense, but in truth it refers to the legend that barrels of brandy had been hidden in a village pond (most often The Crammer in Devizes). The smugglers were retrieving it one night when the moon was full and the skies cloudless. As they were doing so the excisemen appeared and demanded to know what they were doing. Thinking quickly, the smugglers noticed that the moon reflected upon the surface of the water and told the excisemen that they were trying to rake in a round cheese, pointing to the moon's reflection. The excisemen laughed at the apparent stupidity of these naïve locals and went on their way, but the smugglers were anything but silly and were able to retrieve their illicit French brandy from under the noses of the king's men.

Meanwhile, the people of Aldbourne are known as Dabchicks. The story here (or at least one version of it) is that one day a strange bird landed in the

The Crammer, Devizes.

Above left: Moonrakers plaque.

Above right: A Dabchick. (JJ Jarrison)

village pond. Unable to identify this new visitor, the villagers went to the oldest inhabitant and brought him to the pond in a wheelbarrow to gain his advice. He said that the bird was a dabchick, and since then the name stuck. It apparently used to be the custom of the rival village of Ramsbury to tie a dead dabchick to any cart passing through to Aldbourne as a cruel taunt (although more cruel to the poor dabchick than to the people).

The people of Bradford on Avon have two traditional nicknames. The first of these is Gudgeon, owing to the fish weathervane installed atop the former town lock-up on the bridge. The second name is Snuffy, and is said to be due to the polluted water and air that once affected the town due to all the industrial mills and factories nearby.

Pond at Aldbourne. (Nick MacNeill)

Fish weathervane at
Bradford-on-Avon.
(Jaggery)

Knob atop Trowbridge
Blind House.
(Ruth Riddle)

At Trowbridge, the name Knob is customary from the stone ball atop the
blind-house (gaol). Similarly, the villagers of Potterne are known as Lambs as an
ironic twist on the tradition that the people of Potterne were anything but lambs –
instead they had a reputation for working hard, drinking hard, and fighting hard.
It seems that the people of Wiltshire were a fierce breed, for almost all instance of
the nicknames are followed by stories of bitter rivalries between adjacent towns
and vicious fights.

43

Highwaymen and Highwaywomen

Like many places, Wiltshire is no stranger to stories of highwaymen, and close to the village of Bulkington is Dick Turpin's Stone. This memorial was said to be a fitting marker to the demise of the famed highwayman, being as though it was situated in an 'evil-smelling ditch that receives the drainage of the neighbouring pigsties'. The stone apparently carried the inscription 'Dick Turpin's dead and gone/This stone's set up to think upon'. However, the inscription, even in 1908, was badly eroded and the only word that could be identified was 'Turpin'. 'Brake-loads of Wiltshire archaeologists have visited the spot in summer,' writes Charles G. Harper, 'braving typhoid fever, have descended into the ditch and sought to unravel the mystery of this Sphinx: without result'.

One of the more famous of Wiltshire's highwaymen was Thomas Boulter, said to have been as notorious as Dick Turpin. He began terrorising the countryside of Wiltshire in 1775 until he was caught and sentenced to hang after venturing to

Robber's Stone, Imber.
(Hugh Chevallier)

York. He was pardoned after agreeing to join the king's army, but deserted and was later recaptured and sent to the gallows in 1778.

Near to Imber is a memorial known as the Robber's Stone to mark 'the awful end of Benjamin Colclough', a highwayman who fell dead on the spot in an attempt to escape his captors after robbing Mr Dean of Imber on the evening of 21 October 1839. The stone informs us that his body was buried at Chitterne 'without Funeral Rites' whereas his three companions, Thomas Saunderes, George Waters and Richard Harris, were captured and sentenced to fifteen years' transportation at the Devizes Quarter Sessions.

Wiltshire also had a highwaywoman in Mary Sandall of Baverstock, who seems to have been rather unfortunate in her choice of career. Dressing as a man, she held up just one person before being caught and sentenced to death, although the sentence was later reduced.

44

Ruins and Relics

Aside from the stone circles and ancient barrows, Wiltshire is also home to a number of impressive ruins from the not-so-distant past. Within the grounds of Clarendon Park are the remains of Clarendon Palace, dating back to Henry II. Both he and his later successor, Henry III, converted the park into a royal residence and built a substantial stone palace and chapel. The palace was a favoured residence of subsequent kings, but by 1500 it had begun to fall into disrepair and its importance dwindled over the following century. After the execution of Charles I in 1649, the palace was confiscated by parliament and later entered into the hands of minor noblemen after the Restoration in 1660. By the time the present Clarendon Park was created in the eighteenth century, the palace had become a ruin.

The ruins of Wardour Castle met with a similar fate. Built in the 1390s on the permission of Richard II, the castle passed into the hands of the Arundell family following its confiscation from the original inheritors during the Wars of the Roses. It was confiscated by the Crown again in 1552 when Sir Thomas Arundell was executed for treason, but was purchased back by his son in 1570. The Arundells retained hold of the castle until the English Civil Wars. Taking the side of the Royalist cause, a later Sir Thomas departed to fight for the king's

Clarendon Palace ruins. (David Martin)

army, leaving behind his sixty-one-year-old wife and twenty-five men to defend the castle. However, a large Parliamentarian army arrived and laid siege to the building, threatening to destroy it completely unless it was handed over. After five days, Lady Arundell surrendered, and soon after Sir Thomas was killed in battle. His son, Henry, re-took the castle after a bitter siege in late 1643, but in doing so it was rendered uninhabitable, and it was left to fall into ruins.

In Bradenstoke once stood an Augustinian priory dedicated to St Mary and founded in 1142. It grew in importance and wealth over the following centuries, coming to own great tracts of land across nine different counties by the fourteenth century. Like many religious houses, Bradenstoke Priory did not escape the Dissolution of the Monasteries and was surrendered in early 1539. The buildings and lands were sold off by the Crown and left to fall into decay.

The Augustinian monks also had a priory at Ivychurch, which was similarly a rich living for those residing there. However, it was hit by the Black Death in the mid-fourteenth century, killing all but one monk. It took another century for the priory to return to its former glory, but was dissolved in 1536. After this, the buildings were converted into a residential house, and over the following centuries was gradually demolished for building material elsewhere. Today, only a small portion of an arch and pillar survive of the priory.

At Monkton Farleigh was a Cluniac Priory of St Mary Magdalene, founded around 1120. A church was added to the site in 1150, and then the whole priory was rebuilt, larger, in the thirteenth century. Like with the others, the priory was dissolved in 1536 and its remains were later incorporated into Monkton Farleigh Manor.

Another impressive ruin is that of St Leonard's Church at Sutton Veny. Originally built in the twelfth century, it underwent extensive rebuilds in later

Old Wardour Castle. (Michael Dibb)

Above: Undercroft of Bradenstoke Abbey. (Rodhullandemu)

Right: Bradenstoke Abbey ruins. (Rick Crowley)

Below: Monkton Farleigh Manor. (Eirian Evans)

years, and was then 'restored' in 1831. However, the soft ground underneath the church had been causing problems to the stability and safety of the building almost from the moment it was built, and in 1866 it was decided it would be better to build a new church on higher ground nearby. The old church was not declared as redundant until 1970, although much of the building was in a ruinous condition.

'New' St John the Evangelist's Church. (Peter Wood)

45

White Horses of Wiltshire

Just as famous as the ancient stone monuments are Wiltshire's multiple white horses – at least eleven in total, although several have since disappeared. The one at Alton Barnes dates to around 1812 when a local gentleman farmer paid for it to be dug into the hillside.

The Hackpen Hill White Horse is a little later, dating from 1838. However, it is said to give rise to the expression 'as different as chalk and cheese' on account of the fact that Hackpen Hill divides the chalk hills to the south and the rich dairy pastures to the north.

Tan Hill also had a white horse, which for many decades became lost and was thought to be mythical in its own right. However, in 1975 it was rediscovered, although has since been lost once again. This horse was rumoured to wander down to a local pond to drink when All Cannings' Church struck midnight; perhaps he decided to wander on a bit further and that is why he can no longer be seen at Tan Hill anymore!

Perhaps the most famous, and the oldest, of all of Wiltshire's white horses is the Westbury White Horse. The first mention of this horse was in 1742, in which

Alton Barnes White Horse. (Rude Health)

a Reverend Wise states that it had been cut into the hillside around a century earlier as a memorial to the local people. Then, in 1778 this original white horse was removed and another one cut in its place. The present horse dates to 1873, when the second horse was restored and reshaped. In the 1950s, and again in the 1990s, the chalk was covered in concrete to reduce the expense of maintenance. Like with his counterpart at Tan Hill, the Westbury White Horse is said to get up and find a pond to drink in when the local clock strikes twelve. Another legend is that it actually dates to the victory of King Alfred over the Danes in AD 878 (perhaps originally as a dragon than a horse), but has been remodelled over the last 1,000 years or so.

A little younger than Westbury is the Cherhill White Horse, cut in 1780 by a doctor from Calne, apparently on orders shouted though a loudhailer. Originally, the eye was made of glass until the 1970s, but the bottles from which it was made had a habit of disappearing, and so a stone and concrete eye has been added. It is also thought by some that Dr Alsop's horse replaced one on the site from an earlier date.

Westbury White Horse. (Neil Kemp)

Cherhill White Horse. (David Howard)

The Broad Town White Horse was cut by a local landowner in 1864, whereas Marlborough's one was cut in 1804 by the pupils of a local school, and has since undergone much restoration and reshaping.

Both Pewsey and Devizes can lay claim to two white horses. At Devizes, the original one was cut in 1845 beneath Oliver's Castle, but later was abandoned and left to turf over. However, in 1999 a new one was cut around a mile east to mark the millennium, and thus became the newest addition to Wiltshire's heard. Unusually, this horse faces right – one of just four in the whole of Britain to do so. Similarly, Pewsey's original horse is thought to date to the late eighteenth century, but fell into neglect and was lost after a few decades. However, a new one was cut beside the old one in 1937 to mark the coronation of George VI.

Right: Marlborough White Horse. (Michael Dibb)

Below: Pewsey White Horse. (Detmar Owen)

Both Rockley and Inkpen Hill once bore white horses, but both of these have been completely lost.

The tradition of chalk carvings has been one that has been maintained in Wiltshire, and has been used to mark the county's long-standing military history. As a result, soldiers of the New Zealand Expeditionary Force stationed at Bulford at the end of the First World War cut a large kiwi into a local hillside in 1919. This was the initiative of the officers in an attempt to quell a rebellion when troop ships were not forthcoming to transport the soldiers back home and they became restless. Needing to find some way to keep the men busy, the Canterbury, Otago and Engineers Battalions were given the task of cutting the 1.5-acre kiwi based upon a design by Sergeant-Major Percy Blenkarne. After the war, it became a memorial to the New Zealand soldiers lost in the war, and was maintained by local villagers. He was camouflaged in 1940 to prevent German bombers using it as a navigational aid, but was restored by a local Scout troop in 1948.

Bulford kiwi.
(Jonathanjosh1)

Map of Australia.
("MO" Maurice S)

Meanwhile, at Compton Chamberlayne a chalk outline of Australia has been carved as a memorial to the Australian soldiers camped nearby during the First World War.

Finally, near Fovant are a series of regimental badges cut by soldiers awaiting transport to France in 1916. Today, nine badges still survive and are listed as war memorials, with additional ones added in 1950 and 1970. A large poppy was also cut in 2016 to mark the centenary of the first badge (that of the 6th (City of London) Battalion, London Regiment (City of London Rifles)) being made in 1916. Originally, there were at least eleven more badges here, but have all been lost.

Nearby, but separate from the Fovant Badges, is the regimental badge of the Royal Warwickshire Regiment at Sutton Down.

Above: Fovant Badges. (Marchibald.fly)

Below: Royal Warwickshire Regiment badge. ("MO" Maurice S)

46

Wiltshire Customs and Superstitions

Many folk-customs and superstations exist in Wiltshire from time immemorial when magic and supernatural interventions were more readily believed in. For example, if a lit candle guttered, forming a ridge of wax down the side, it was called a 'winding-sheet' and a death was imminent in that household. However, if the wick sparked a little, then whoever was sitting closest would receive an important letter in the post; a large spark, on the other hand, warned of thieves.

The Christmas pudding was also something to be treated with care – if it broke before being eaten, then a death would befall the head of the household. Another death omen was to sit in a recently vacated chair; doing so meant that the sitter would follow the previous occupant to the grave. A sugary treat known as a Twelfth Cake was also traditional, and inside would be placed a bean, a coin, a ring and a thimble. Other foodstuffs with supernatural properties included wedding cakes; newlyweds would place a slice under their pillow to dream upon on their wedding night.

Cutting the Twelfth Cake. (*Parley's Magazine*)

The question of finding who to marry was also the subject of divination in northern parts of Wiltshire in the years before the English Civil War. In a large house, after the day's work had been done and the evening meal eaten, the maids would assemble around the hearth and spread the ashes. Taking up a stick, they would each make streaks through the ashes, with each streak signifying a future husband. The men servants would then do likewise, and through this they would discover who they should each marry.

If a piece of coal jumps out of the fire, then it should be examined (once cool) to determine if it more closely resembled the shape of a coffin, a purse or a cradle; death, riches or long-life would be foretold by whichever shape it was. Wiltshire folk also assigned the traditional magpie rhyme to crows. Similarly, the popular weather rhyme Red Sky at Night had its own particular version unique to Wiltshire, based upon rainbows:

> The rainbow in th' marnin'
> Gies the shepherd warnin'
> To car' his girt cwoat on his back;
> The rainbow at night
> Is the shepherd's delight,
> For then no girt cwoat will he lack.

Rainbow at Great Durnford. (Peter)

However, no Wiltshire folk should take the first look at a new moon through a window, for doing so is an ill omen. On the contrary, however, luck could be achieved by carrying a 'cramp bone', which had the added bonus of warding off rheumatism. A cricket in the house was also a very good omen, but the luck would reverse if the creature was killed.

Cats born in May were considered to be worthless, unable to catch neither mice nor rats, but instead will bring snakes and slow worms into the house. These poor kittens were held in great contempt, and over the border in Hampshire such kittens were immediately killed as recently as the mid to late nineteenth century.

Meanwhile, at Lonbridge Deverill was an old wall known as the Jew's Wall, and it was foretold that when the wall fell it would mark the demise of the Marquisate of Bath.

Shrove Tuesday was a day of peculiar local customs and perhaps the strangest of all was that of Clipping of the Church at Hill Deverill, when around 200 people would circle the church (presumably at Longbridge Deverill) holding hands and then assemble on the Common and gather up stones to throw at the houses of unpopular people.

St Peter and St Paul's Church, Longbridge Deverill. (Peter Wood)

Image Credits

Public Domain – **Immanuel Giel:** Church in Avebury 12. **Arpingstone:** Eilmers. flight.arp. **Derek.hill:** GrovelyWoods1. **Serendigity:** Old Sarum Aerial; Stonehenge From the Air. **Rodw:** Barge Inn at Seend Cleeve. **Neil Kemp:** WestburyWhiteHorseRepainted. **"MO" Maurice S:** Hurdcott ANZAC Day Ceremony 2019 [Australia]; Hurdcott ANZAC Day Ceremony 2019 [Badge]. A History, Military and Municipal, of the Ancient Borough of the Devizes p.128; Salisbury Plain p.217, 223. Merry's Museum, Parley's Magazine p.29.

CC-BY 2.0 (https://creativecommons.org/licenses/by/2.0/) – ©**Odd Wellies:** Church and the Bristol Cross at Stourhead-2. ©**Matt Brown:** A strange tale of dropping down dead. ©**Peter:** Great Durnford with rainbow.

CC-BY-SA 2.0 (https://creativecommons.org/licenses/by-sa/2.0/) – ©**Peter Trimming:** St.Mary & St.Melor, Amesbury, Wiltshire. ©**Vieve Forward:** On the ramparts of Ringsbury Camp, near Dogridge, Purton; Beech plantation, Hackpen Hill. ©**M. J. Richardson:** Boscombe Down Airfield and Amesbury. ©**Brian Robert Marshall:** Wilts & Berks canal, near Royal Wootton Bassett. ©**David Howard:** Cley Hill, Sturford; The White Horse, Cherhill. ©**Elliott Simpson:** Heading east out of Box Tunnel. ©**Maurice Pullin:** 2010: Barbed wire fence on Cow Down. ©**Nick MacNeill:** Village pond at Aldbourne, Wilts. ©**Mark Percy:** The Devil's Den. ©**Chris Andrews:** Grey Wethers, Fyfield Down. ©**Jaggery:** Former chapel and lockup on Town Bridge, Bradford-on-Avon; Chaps Barber Shop in Malmesbury. ©**Michael Dibb:** Old Sarum [4]; Oliver's Castle; Old Wardour Castle [5]; Marlborough features [4]; A circular walk around Horton and Bourton [54]. ©**John Potts:** Egbert's Stone. ©**Jim Osley:** Portico, "White Hart Hotel", Salisbury; Clock tower, Fisherton Street, Salisbury. ©**Derek Harper:** Track, Four Sisters; Clearing, Grovely Woods. ©**Hugh Chevallier:** The robber's stone, Imber. ©**Stuart Logan:** The Clock House. ©**James Harrison:** View down towards Priory Farm, Maiden Bradley, Wiltshire. ©**Steve Roberts:** Old Court House, St John's Street, Malmesbury. ©**David Martin:** Footpath on Laverstock Down; Clarendon Palace ruins. ©**Steve Daniels:** Silbury Hill from the A4; Littlecote House. ©**Ruth Riddle:** The Blind House. ©**Chris Talbot:** Pewsey – Phoenix Square. ©**Richard Humphrey:** Church of St John the Baptist in Pewsey. ©**Wayland Smith:** River Key. ©**Rick Crowley:** Bradenstoke Abbey. ©**Peter Wood:** The Church of St John the Evangelist at Sutton Veny; The Church of St Peter and St Paul at Longbridge Deverill. ©**Eirian Evans:** A peep at Monkton Farleigh Manor. ©**Neil Owen:** A cave for visitors?. ©**Lewis Clarke:** Bournemouth, View over Kinson. ©**Rob Farrow:** Tyger victim. ©**Tim Heaton:** Church of St Michael and All Angels, Urchfont. ©**Rude Health:** White Horse Near Milk Hill. ©**Colin Smith:** Hungerford – St Lawrence's Church.

Select Bibliography

A History, Military and Municipal, of the Ancient Borough of The Devizes (London: Longman, Brown & Co., 1859).

Ancient Aliens, S.12 Ep.3 'The Mystery of Rudloe Manor' (2017). [TV Programme] History Channel: 12 May 2017.

Brighton, Simon, Welbourn, Terry, *Echoes of the Goddess* (Hersham: Ian Allen Publishing, 2010).

Britten, James (ed.), *Remaines of Gentilisme and Judaisme by John Aubrey, R.S.S. 1686-87* (London: W. Satchell, Peyton, And Co., 1881).

Britton, John, *The Beauties of England and Wales* [Vol.15 Wiltshire] (London: J. Harris, 1814).

Britton, John, *The Beauties of Wiltshire* [Vol.2] (London, 1801).

Burl, Aubrey, *Prehistoric Henges* (Princes Risborough: Shire Publications, 1997 [1991]).

Choice Notes from 'Notes and Queries' [Vol.2] (London: Bell and Daldy, 1859).

The *Cincinnati Enquirer*, 23 May 1955.

Dakota Farmers' Leader, 22 December 1911.

Defence Equipment & Support, *Corsham Tunnels: A Brief History* (Corsham: Information Systems and Services).

Eagle River Review, 1 December 1911.

Folklore [Vol.26, Issue 2], 1915.

Foot, David (ed.), *Wiltshire Mysteries* (Bodmin: Bossiney Books, 1989)

Wainwright, Geoffrey, *The Henge Monuments* (London: Thames and Hudson, 1989).

Geelong Advertiser, 15 June 1912.

The *Gentleman's Magazine* [Vol.274], 1893.

The *Gentleman's Magazine* [Vol.277], 1894.

Genzmer, Herbert, Hellenbrand, Ulrich, *Mysteries of the World* (Bath: Parragon Books, 2011 [2007]).

Goddard, E. H. (ed.), *The Wiltshire Archaeological & Natural History Magazine* [Vol.43] (Devizes: C. H. Woodward, 1927).

Gomme, George Laurence (ed.), *The Gentleman's Magazine Library: Popular Superstitions* (London: Elliot Stock, 1884).

Hadingham, Evan, *Circles and Standing Stones* (London: William Heinemann Ltd, 1977 [1975]).

Harper, Charles G., *Half-Hours With the Highwaymen* [Vol.2] (London: Chapman & Hall, 1908).

Harper, Charles G., *The Smugglers* (London: Chapman & Hall, 1909).

Harris, James, *Copies of The Epitaphs in Salisbury Cathedral, &c* (Salisbury: Brodie and Dowding, 1825).

Hulme, Frederick Edward, *The Town, College, and Neighbourhood of Marlborough* (London: Edward Stanford, 1881).

Marsh, A. E. W., *A History of the Borough and Town of Calne* (Calne: Robert S. Heath, 1904).

Nature, 31 October 1901.

Noyes, Ella, *Salisbury Plain* (London: J. M. Dent & Sons, 1913).

Poor-Poore Family Association, *The Poor-Poore Family Gathering at Newburyport, Mass., Sept. 14th, 1881* [Vol.1] (New York: S. W. Green's Son, 1881).

Puttick, Betty (ed.), *Supernatural England* (Newbury: Countryside Books, 2003 [2002]).

Smith, W. Francis, *A School History of Wiltshire* (Calne: R. S. Heath, 1907).

Sone, George, *New Curiosities of Literature* [Vol.1] (London: E. Churton, 1847).

Swindon Advertiser, 13 July 2016 [Online]

Taunton Courier and Western Advertiser, 13 September 1916.

The Times, 9 February 1960.

Timbs, John, Gunn, Alexander, *Abbeys, Castles, and Ancient Halls of England and Wales* [Vol.2] (London: Frederick Warne and Co., 1872).

Townsend, Joseph, *A Dissertation on the Poor Laws* (1786).

Walker, Charles, *The Atlas of Occult Britain* (Twickenham: The Hamlyn Publishing Group, 1987).

Wiltshire Archaeological and Natural History Society, *The Wiltshire Archaeological and Natural History Magazine* [Vol.13] (Devizes: H., F. & E. Bull, 1872).

Wiltshire Archaeological and Natural History Society, *The Wiltshire Archaeological and Natural History Magazine* [Vol.17] (Devizes: H. F. & E. Bull, 1878).

Wiltshire Notes & Queries, March 1893.

Woodcock, Alex, Oakley, Theresa, 'The Romanesque Corbel-table at St John's, Devizes, and its Sheela-na-gig', in The Wiltshire Archaeological and Natural History Society, *The Wiltshire Archaeological and Natural History Magazine* [Vol.99] (Salisbury: Salisbury Printing Co. Ltd, 2006).